How to Turn Your Man Into a
Red Hot Lover

For Woman Only

By
Mike Riley

Published, printed and bound
by Mike Riley
Aboard the Beau Soleil somewhere on the Seven Seas

And
For sale by Amazon

http://www.amazon.com/author/mike.riley

ISBN# 978-0-9895532-0-9

sailingbooks@rocketmail.com

Table of Contents

Preface

I spent the early days of my life sailing around the world alone on a 24' sailboat. I visited every continent and many countries; and I seemed to find a lady in each. They all taught me things about myself and about how to please them. I was a slow learner so they had to teach me over and over again. Most of my lessons I remembered and now after keeping them to myself all these years, I pass them on to you in written form before age catches up to me and I start to forget. It would be a shame to lose all that information!

Men. If you made a mistake and only now realize that this is a book for women, please don't use any of the techniques in this book to weave a spell over women. That would be a very dishonest thing to do. The purpose of this book is to promote the ability to love well, both sexually and emotionally.

Women. The above holds true for you as well. Men are actually fragile creatures; their ids can be broken so easily. If you want to use our bodies for your pleasure, at least try to love us a little, too.

The names of the girls have been changed, not that it would have made much difference. They are all as old as I am now. Only the lawyers care. But the names do not matter, only my wonderful memories of them.

Introduction

Let's face it. As men get older, things just don't work as well as they used to, not that we don't try harder. The older we get the harder we try. Not that it does us much good, normally. Good thing they invented Viagra and all those similar drugs. But it still isn't the same. Our legs don't tingle when we kiss, our knees don't knock at just the touch of a pretty girl, thank god that our tongues don't become inoperable at the thought of conversing with a girl we like. It doesn't matter if we can use a drug to get it up or not, it still isn't the same. And what happens if your guy is taking so many drugs that the doctors have forbidden him to take Viagra? What then? Is there no hope? Is sex a thing of the past?

It does not have to be so. The human body is an extremely complicated network of nerves many of which become active during sex. When we men were teenagers, we all heard stories of 'spots' that would turn on a girl. Places that just a touch would make her fall into your arms, panting, with her eyes closed. Most of them were just that, stories. We never thought that we might one day need to know where our male 'spots' were, or rather our wives, girlfriends, lovers and sweethearts would need to know. We males have 'turn on spots,' too you know. Or maybe you didn't? We do. Read on! Your man's sex life is about to get better, and so is yours, ladies!

It has long been known that many women stay in abusive relationships just because the sex is good. She really has great orgasms with him. He may beat her, abuse her, vocally and physically but she stays with him. Equally well, many men will stay with the same wife for years even after all the love is long gone just because she can really ring his bell. She knows how to not just get him off, but how to make him come like he has never come before. All heterosexual women need this knowledge. Especially those women who have a husband, sweetheart, lover or boyfriend who is over 60 years of age. When we men were younger, nature made sure we were always ready to go at the drop of a hat or at least a skirt. Sadly, it isn't that way anymore. Now we need help. You ladies have to push our buttons to get us going. For girls who like to play on both sides of the sheet, there is plenty for you in this book also. In order to turn men on, we have to teach them to turn on his girl. Believe me, there is plenty that he doesn't know. Maybe somethings you aren't sure about too.

We are all taught, endlessly it seems, that men lose testosterone as they age. Testosterone is part of the process male's bodies use to attain an erection. It is true that some men lose testosterone as they age, especially as they pass their 60th birthday but it isn't true that age is making them lose that testosterone. Most often, the cause is medicines they are taking or diseases they have caught. In any case, it isn't how much testosterone a man has in his blood in a doctor's office. It is how much he has when he is in bed with you. Testosterone is a hormone that is released by the testes when a man either smells an ovulating female or is visually or tactilely stimulated. If a girl wants her man to be harder, sexier, more aggressive, more like he used to be, she has but to increase his testosterone level! How? Well, that is what this book is all about!

The fact is you can make your man as hard as he ever was when he was twenty. Back then, we didn't have to worry. Back then it wasn't a problem. Actually, back then, it was a problem; it seemed he was always hard. He was hard when you went to sleep, when you woke up, when he woke you up in the middle of the night, twice, when he got home, when he went off to work. There is only so much sex a girl can have before she starts having problems walking! But that was back then. Now he is getting older. In fact, he is over 60. Is everything over? Or is there help for the older women of the world? Women over 60 are just reaching their sexual peak! They are! Really! No one knew that, before the use of lubricants became common. Everyone thought older gals dried up and forgot about sex. Forgot about sex! My god! What lies they tell! You don't have to worry about getting pregnant now; your guys will actually cuddle with you and talk over the day! And miracles of miracles, their cuddles aren't foreplay! How marvelous! It puts you in the driver's seat. Women rule!

If you can learn to turn your man on, on command, you will be in the driver's seat. Your 60 plus guy will be so thankful! He will wine and dine you like he did when you both first met! Life will be good, hell, life will be perfect! You can do it. An old girl can always learn a few new tricks! Of course, you might be shy. All girls are shy; it is in their nature. You might be overly shy.

How can you try something new in bed? Will he think you have been learning from other men? Will he get that angry look in his eyes? Will he jump out of bed and snarl at you? Well, actually, you have been learning from another man, me! You can show him the cover of the book. That is proof enough. Don't let him read it. You don't want him to know what you are going to be doing to him! Let it be a surprise, a surprise when his package grows to an astounding size! The hell with shyness. Do you want to get laid or not? Do you want to lie there afterwards without a thought in your brain; just filled with incredible pleasure. Do you want him to do it to you two, three, four times a night? Men can perform incredibly after they have passed their 60th birthday. You just have to know which buttons to push!

Chapter One
How Men Work

Men are complicated. Very. They say that women are complicated. They don't know what they are talking about. Women are basic. Straightforward. Simple. They want respect, they want to be appreciated, they want to be adored. That's it. Simple. Men aren't. Simple, that is. Men want their fellow men to respect them. They want the women in their lives to obey them. They want a profession of some kind that they feel challenged by but are capable of performing. They want to pursue a woman or women. And on top of all, they want victory. They want to fight the good fight and end up victorious. Most likely he doesn't even know he wants these things. Men are very complicated. God made Adam first. By the time He made Eve, He had all the kinks worked out!

Your man over 60 has had many victories. It doesn't seem to matter. He will still want more. When his team loses on a game on television, it matters to him. Actually, it matters to you, too. There have been many well documented studies that show that when men watch a sexually explicit movie, they become aroused; however their testosterone doesn't peak till 60 to 90 minutes after the end of the movie. Equally well, when their team loses on Monday Night Football, their testosterone is at its lowest 60 to 90 minutes later. If you are after some action in the sack, pay attention to what is happening in his life unless you want just another ho hum lay. The more testosterone he has running around in his blood stream the harder he will be, the bigger he will be and the longer he will last. It doesn't matter how many kisses you give him, what techniques you might use on him, if his team lost, you are fighting a lost cause. You might well think that you are more important than any stupid game on the idiot box, and you will be right. If you ask him, he will agree. He will tell you how much he loves you, but if his team lost, it's a burst balloon. The hormones just aren't there. It isn't his fault. Men are complicated.

Your man will like to look at porn. Don't get upset. Don't throw away his magazines, don't delete his computer files. He doesn't know why he likes looking at porn. He doesn't know that he is appeasing the immature id of his personality by pretending to pursue women. There is a lot of power in checking a girl out, completely out, and then turning the page, ignoring her and checking out another. He is not comparing the women in his porn to you. His id is hunting, deciding who he is going to have for the night. Yes, they are just images. Yes, he is going to spend the night with you. He doesn't realize what he is doing. He is fulfilling his primal urges. When they handed out insightfulness, men were last in line. Some women try to compete with the porn. They don their sexiest clothes and accidentally glide past their guy bending this way and that to show off their charms. This works quite well for getting his attention, not so good on getting him to wait till his testosterone has peaked. That is very important. If you are going to do it, might as well do it when he is at his readiest. When men are busy checking out women, real or not, their testosterone peaks 30 minutes after he has made his choice. After he has picked you. So when he turns off the computer, accidentally happen by with your skimpiest clothes on. Let him pick you and then busy yourself for 30 minutes. Take a shower, anything. If you are going to get laid it might as well be by a testosterone laden male.

Men love to give orders and they love even more to be obeyed. It is easy to say that it makes him feel like a man if you obey his every wish, but far truer is to say obeying him spikes his testosterone. Obedience is a bit quicker to get a response than porn. There is a small spike 15 to 30 minutes after each time you kowtow to him. It is a small response but they are cumulative. It doesn't seem to matter if you gave him orders all day long; if you continually ignored his comments. Start obeying when he turns off his porn. Start obeying 30 minutes before he plans to be in bed. That should get enough testosterone in his system to make you think he is, well not a teenager, maybe a 40 year old.

Many 60+ year olds aren't working anymore. That doesn't mean he has given up his desire for a career. Well, not so much a career as much as something to occupy his time. It might be golf, it might be working with wood in the garage, it might even be sailing around the world. Whatever it is, keep half an ear open when he talks about it. When he is happy with his performance in the 'workplace' his testosterone will go up. Tests attempting to determine when and by how much his testosterone will go up are inconclusive. Or we are asking the wrong questions. It does go up, that we know. Up is good, right!

Many men aren't particularly social. But at the same time, they crave being accepted by their tribe of fellow men. When they feel like they are accepted, even if it is only by the other old coots down at the senior center, they become better lovers about an hour afterwards. If they wander down to the senior center on Tuesdays, pencil Tuesday afternoons in for an afternoon delight! Yes, men are very complicated. But women are more than capable of handling them. And you do want to. We are talking about getting a bit of loving here! Actually, no. We are talking about getting a whole lot of loving, especially Tuesday afternoons!

This book is about maximizing testosterone in your lover's bloodstream when you want to make love and balancing it with oxytocin so that he will last all night long. You should have had this book years ago when it could have really helped you understand your mate and/or lover, but I was still learning this stuff myself. Nevertheless, here it is at last. Your golden years really are going to be worth living!

Yes, men are complicated, but you women are more than capable of directing them and never letting them know that you are. Not that you are bossy or tricky or anything. You are just trying to get laid!

Loni

I met Loni on Kosrae which is an island in the Republic of the Eastern Carolines in Micronesia. It is an island rich in history. Millennia ago, Kosrae was the island of love in the days before the missionaries came. It was the island where all the chiefs and kings, in island groups across the Pacific, sent their soon to be wives to learn the secrets of making love. Now days, away from the town, old ways die hard. Select girls can still attend the school. *(More information can be found in Mike Riley's book, "Edens I have Known and Loved" available on Kindle, Amazon, and on board the good ketch, Beau Soleil, if we ever happen to be in the same port!)*

Loni was in her last year in the sex school and was looking for someone to do her homework on and in I sailed. Not that I minded! She was a beautiful Polynesian girl. She didn't speak much English but that didn't seem to matter. In the physical way of Polynesian women, if I wasn't licking in the right spot, she grabbed my hair and twisted and pulled until I was doing it right! Language really wasn't necessary! When she did things to me I was too busy screaming to pay much attention. Good thing I stayed for a month and she had plenty of time for repeated lessons! I hope she passed her tests! If I was grading her she would have gotten straight A's!

Loni taught me that the woman's body had a multitude of erogenous zones. She said the Polynesian name for each but it is hard to remember when she was yanking at my hair! She showed me lots of zones on my body, too. More than I ever realized.

What a wonderful month! I would have stayed longer, but actually I was worn out! I needed to escape to the sea! But I learned a lot. Many of the more exotic erogenous zones described in this book came from Loni. You have to believe her. After all, she went to school! Plus, they really work!

Chapter Two
Foreplay

Men's bodies are loaded with telltale parts which indicate how much testosterone is running through their bloodstream. But sex isn't just about testosterone. There are other hormones running through his body especially during foreplay. And we do like foreplay, don't we? Now that you both are older, you have time to take the time to really enjoy getting yourself turned on and getting him to his peak of readiness. It is a mistake during foreplay to concentrate on his penis. Men are already too fixated on it. Sex after 60 is the time to start to explore other parts of his body and how they can make him into, not only a better lover, but a verifiable Don Juan! *(For more information about hormones, check out my companion book, 'How to Turn your Woman into a Raving Nymphomaniac, For Men Only! Yes, it is for women too, but saying men only is a trick Mark Twain used in promoting his book, Huckleberry Finn!))*

Some women really enjoy having their nipples played with. Some can even become so aroused that they orgasm, just with nipple play. On the other hand almost all men enjoy having their nipples played with, whether they know it or not. Some men can also orgasm if you touch nothing but their nipples. *(What fun is that?)*

People often wonder how many erogenous zones there are. The answer is easy. Two. And the most important is the brain. Yes, yes. The genitals are the other. A quadriplegic can orgasm with out any help from his or her brain; we know because the nerves of the lower body are cut off from the head. Both sexes can have children without any help from the brain. Irregardless, the brain is far more important erogenous zone. The other so called erogenous zones: the bridge of the nose, the lips, the sides of the neck below the ears, the tuft of hair at the nape of the neck, the breasts, the nipples, the hollow in the rib cage on the right side, the upper part of the belly button, the sides of the stomach below the ribs, the clitoris, the anus, the perineum, the prostate in males, the G, U, A, K, and P spots in women's vaginas, the inside of the thighs, the inside of the knees, the bottoms of the feet, the longest toe and the ring finger; they all depend on the brain to function. These spots release oxytocin when massaged, touched or pinched. Oxytocin is a powerful hormone which activates the pleasure zones in the brain, blocks pain and it is also the hormone that readies the vagina and clitoris for intercourse. In males, it activates the pleasure zones of the brain and directs the testes and the hypothalamus gland to release testosterone.

Men are complicated. Men's nipples are exceptionally complicated. When they are played with, they signal the brain to release oxytocin, the pleasure hormone. However when the nipples get hard and elongated, it is testosterone making them become active. This is great for women. A quick glance at a man without a shirt will tell her the amount of testosterone running around inside his body. A normal amount will leave the nipples ever so slightly projected from his areola. A less than normal amount of testosterone and his nipples will be flush, not projecting at all. A man with a lot of testosterone running around his bloodstream, getting everything read for love, will have nipples that project from the areola like a woman's but of course, smaller, and appear darker in color as they are all puckered up. There you go. I bet you are going to have fun the next time you are at the beach! Go with your girlfriends. You could point out men walking by and say, "Get a load of those nipples!" When you think about it, a man's nipples are the only other part of his body that becomes erect and since they are not used to feed babies, then like the clitoris they exist only for pleasure.

Nipples are fun during foreplay. They react much like a clitoris. Be very gentle at first. A soft circular motion with a moistened finger, then a rare flick with a fingernail, then as he hardens, twist them like an old fashioned TV set, a rapid series of flicks with fingernails, pull them out and twist hard, and when he is really hard, pinch with fingernails. My goodness, I better take a cold shower. I might not be able to continue! As you play with his nipples, they are causing oxytocin to be released which not only gives his brain pleasure

(Which it is all about. We are trying to turn the brain on. The brain is in charge of telling the testes to releasing testosterone which is what this whole foreplay thing is all about.) But also the oxytocin deadens the pain the more he is turned on. When you are pinching with your fingernails, he isn't in pain. He isn't! Believe me! If his body hasn't released enough oxytocin he will complain. Be gentle until you get those nipples to really stick out and then enjoy yourself! Your man will say whatever you are doing isn't making his nipples feel better. Of course not. Explain to him that nipple play is about making his testicles tighten and his penis thicken and become longer. The same as when your nipples are played with, you become wetter and your cervix, g spot and clitoris grow larger as your vagina wakes up. Oxytocin also creates a rosé flush on your chest just below your neck which is how your mother always knew when you were making out as a teenager!

There is a nerve that leads from the male's nipples directly to his penis. It is fine and dandy to get hormones on your side, but they are slow. Nerves aren't. They are very fast. Nerves are a girl's best friend. The first time Loni bit my nipple with her eye tooth, hard, when I was almost ready to come, I swear, I doubled in girth and increased half again in length. It was the most awesome thing. I couldn't move for ten minutes after. Every nerve in my body was resonating with each other. And none of them had the slightest interest in obeying my mind's commands!

While you are playing with his nipples, reach around and find the last little bit of head hair on his neck. If you can, twist some and twirl it around your finger. Pull. Pull as hard as you want. It doesn't hurt. Try it on yourself right now. The hair on either side hurts, the hair above hurts when pulled but not the little special tuft of hair. If you were Buddhist, you would never cut that little piece of hair. It is by this hair that Buddha pulls you into heaven. And on earth, your girlfriend can have fun turning you on. There are nerves deep inside this area in the neck that lead directly to the Hypothalamus, a gland in the brain that translates signals from the body and then directs the Thalamus to produce the appropriate hormone. The hormones it produces that we are worried about is oxytocin and testosterone. Pulling that little tuft of hair is the fastest way to get your guy on the way to great sex!

The bridge of the nose is an interesting erogenous zone. It is a wonderful zone for releasing tension and for easing sinus congestion. Many nerves run through the area and it is a great place to start foreplay. It will relax your man and he will think that you are just caring for him, instead of believing you have designs on his body! Silly Man! Put your thumb on either side of his nose, just above his eye, below the brow and find a little bump there. Push it, push it hard enough to bend his head backwards and then stroke your fingers down the area below the ear lobes with your other hand.

Many people believe that the ear lobes are an erogenous zone. They aren't. At least they aren't anymore than the tip of your nose or chin. But what is an erogenous zone is the skin just below the ear lobes. Women wear earrings for style and decoration, yes, but also they dangle and tickle this area of skin. Or in a stud, the end of the stud pokes at odd moments. In the past scientists believed that the earrings pulled the lobes of the ear causing the wearer to be in a constant state of sexual awareness. They now know that it wasn't the ear lobes at all. *(Proponents of ear lobes point out the highly developed veins running through the area, which is true. We aren't talking about blood here, we want nerves. Ear lobes are a good indicator of increased arousal as they turn pink when the penis enlarges but they don't make it grow. Besides, if blood flow was so important, why would you constrict the area with a clothes peg which adherents suggest?)*

Push the little spots on either side of the nose and stroke his skin on the opposite side from his ear lobe down to his collarbone. Switch sides every few minutes. When he is relaxed, when his eyes starting to dilate, move your hand from his nose and find the hollow in his rib cage on his right side. *(Your left side, right? Sorry, correct?)* It is next to the sternum, the breastbone, closer to his collar bone than his nipple. Can't find it? Run your hand down on the right side of his breastbone. The ribs will all be in line, like soldiers at attention. One isn't. That is the zone. This is a powerful site. Mystics and primitive peoples believe that taping this spot every other heartbeat will allow you to communicate with your dead ancestors. I don't know if that is right or even if it will work. But I do know that it is a very unusual erogenous zone. Don't expect an instantly erect penis. It isn't that kind of site. It will bring your man into an increased state of awareness. He will be more able to sense what you want for once without you having to tell him. He might even be able to find your clitoris! Just joking, if any guys are reading this. We always know where it is. Damn right! Down there somewhere!

Continue to stroke the skin below his ear and tap his hollow once for each stroke with the pad of your longest finger. Watch his lungs fill with air. Watch his hips thrust forward. After a few minutes, tap his hollow and after tapping lightly glide your finger down his chest and over his nipple on the left side. Every time your fingers slide down the skin below his ear, tap and slide your other hand over his nipple at the same time. If he tries to lift his head to see what is going on, twist your fingers around his tuft of hair at the nape of his neck and pull his head back down. I do hope you have a lot of hands at your command!

Abandon his neck and slide your hand down his chest to his nipples. Circle them lightly around and around. Each time you tap his chest, flick the tip of a nipple with your fingernail, lightly. Later you can get more physical. Don't spend much time with his nipples yet. A few circles, a few flicks each and then move your hand down to his belly button. The erogenous zone here is very small, but worth it. Each time you tap his chest put your finger nail inside the top of his belly button and flick up. *(Long nails are good here!)* There is a little loose fold of skin there; this is the spot you want to flick. It is the same spot where a belly button stud pokes through. Experiment on yourself to determine the right amount of force needed. Too light and nothing will happen. Too hard and he will complain about the pain. Done just right and it will send a little jolt of electricity down to his perineum for each flick. *(The perineum is the area on a man between his testicles and his anus and is a highly sensitive erogenous zone. More later!)* It is difficult to flick the belly button just right but worth it in the end if you can do it properly. When you practice on yourself, you will say, "This Mike Riley is full of

#%&^." Don't judge too early. This is a remarkable site. Give your man a hand job and flick his belly button once for every stroke and when he comes he will shoot with the distance and amount he did when he was 19. Amazing. He will complain about the flicks. He will say it annoys him. Ignore him. Tie him down on the bed if he tries to get away. Try it. It really works!

Move downwards. Slide one hand down the side of his stomach starting from just below his solar plexus, along his rib cage arcing down to his side and back to his pubic hair. This is an incredible erogenous zone. Done properly, *(the amount of force needed is different for each man)* you can make your man come without touching him anywhere else. Older men usually carry a little extra fat around their middle. Be carefully about pushing too hard, you might hurt them. At the same time, take your other hand and starting at the inside of the knee on the same side; softly glide your hand up the inside of his thigh ending just below his testicles just as your other hand has reached his pubic hair. Don't touch the testicles. You want to heat him up, not blast him off!

By this time your guy is going to be half crazy. He will be trying to grab you and throw you on your back and have his way with your little pristine body. Don't let him. Yes, it would be fun. But if you want an exceptional roll in the hay, you have to get his testosterone level even higher. If he is really obstinate, sit on top of him facing his feet, just to give him something to play with. Like car keys for the baby, right?!

A man's testicles are very sensitive. They are especially sensitive to rebound pain, like being kicked or hit with a baseball. Don't think that you can't play with them, after all look how often we are scratching them! Men love their balls fondled! Cup your hand around the base of his testicles. If they are tight to his skin by now, proceed slowly. Circle your thumb and long man finger between his penis and testicles and slowly tighten. You won't hurt him. Tighten until the skin of his scrotum is drum tight and his balls are in the skin above your fingers. Scratch his balls with your fingertips and then lightly tap them with a finger. Again you won't hurt him as long as the testicles can't move back and rebound forward. The rebound is what hurts. If you are into oral, men love to have their ball licked. Don't play with his penis. Don't give him a chance to waste your testosterone. You are doing all the work. You deserve the pleasure of a rock hard, blue ball, enormous hard on!

Before he gets too excited and orgasms without you, slide down to his feet and rub his insteps. This isn't a massage. Stroke them with the back of you fingernails, lightly. You will be able to feel the electricity surging up his legs! Grab the sides of his longest toe, the one next to his big toe. Squeeze the area between the toe's pad and the nail, closer to the pad. Squeeze hard. This will slow down the electricity from his arches and also it sends more testosterone into his system. Turn around, staying on top, grab the tips of his longest fingers between the nail and the pad. Squeeze hard. Again pain in this area will send testosterone flooding into his system.

While you are turned around let him play with your clitoris, or rather not play. Normally the clitoris is hidden under the clitoral hood, invisible. However as you have more oxytocin in your system the hood will retract, the clitoris will elongate and reveal itself as a little pink nub. This is the tip of the head of the clitoris. The shame is this is about as far as most women get. The clitoris can become much longer. It can stick out an inch to an inch and a half from your body, given enough oxytocin and stimulation. The head of the clitoris actually looks a lot like the head of a penis without the pee slit in the middle! To be able to see it in its glory, have him lick your k spots *(More later!)* and as your clitoral hood retracts, have him lick the side of your clitoris. Most men rub the tip of the clitoris. That is like rubbing the tip of his penis. It might get the job down but it is a far cry from rubbing the shaft. Yes, the clitoris has a shaft too. Have him lick from your U spots to your k spots passing lightly over the clitoris. *(Yes, yes, more on these spots later!)* The clitoris will come out of hiding and start to grow. It will pull your inner labia up as it grows and start to open your vagina. Have him lick your clitoris' shaft as it grows. It will really turn him on when you start to writhe and moan at his touch. Your love juices will be laced with oxytocin which will make him even harder when he smells them. When you orgasm, have him suck your clitoris into his mouth as hard as sucking a malt through a straw. No teeth please!

Are you having fun yet? Don't you love foreplay? If he isn't as hard as a rock by now, repeat in areas where you think he was particularly responsive. When you think he is ready, it is time to kiss him, finally. Once you do, he will take it as a signal that it is his turn. You will find that you have lost control! The kiss is a mighty erogenous zone. In a way it is much more personal than making love. Make sure your lips are thoroughly moistened. Approach his mouth slowly and barely touch his lips at first. He will have so much electricity running around his body by now, don't be surprise if you get a little shock. Don't worry, it won't hurt you. Stare at his lips, not his eyes. Let him know that his lips are the sexiest part of his body. This will pay dividends later! Kiss him again. Don't stick your tongue down his throat. Only his lips are the erogenous zone. Stick your tongue in and touch the inside edge of his lips. Don't go past the teeth. Don't forget to breathe. You will be filled with hormones by now and his brain will sense them on your breath and cause him to release even more testosterone! You are really going to get laid, lady!

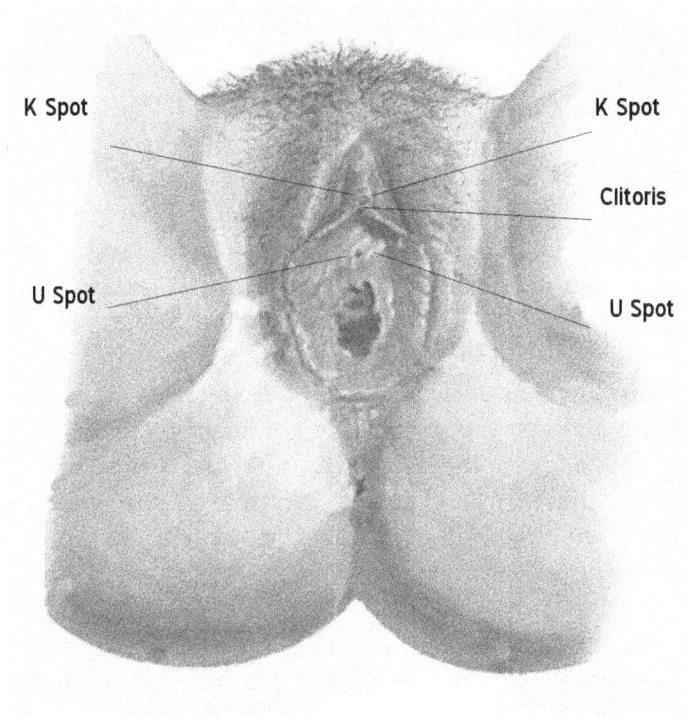

K Spot

K Spot

Clitoris

U Spot

U Spot

Outer Erogenous Zones
In the Female

Nicosia

I met Nicosia in New Caledonia, a French island in the Western South Pacific. She spoke beautiful English. If fact she used to be a translator in Tahiti for important people and companies. She was older than I but that didn't seem to matter. In the practical way of the French, it is assumed that everyone had a lover, whether they were married or not.

Nicosia taught me about rhythm. There is a rhythm to making love. You don't start out too fast or too strong. There should be a building of emotion, of passion, of desire. It should start out in love, in a kiss. Building slowly, it should end with an uncontrollable thrusting into each other's bodies.

Nicosia believed that each time we made love; we should have sex three times. The first was wild and fast, uncontrollable. The second was long and tender and the third was to make love so well that we blew each other's brains apart. To make love well enough, passionately enough, so that at the end we had no choice but to sleep in each other's arms, exhausted.

Nicosia was the first girl I made squirt. *(see Chapter Four)* In the heights of passion she lost her English and would scream in French, not that I minded. I marked it down as foreign language credit!

Chapter Three
Making Love
Part One

Older men don't have the endurance they used to have when they were younger. If you are going to be happy with a quickie, it doesn't matter who is on top or what position you choose. However, now that you both are older and have time on your hands, you might as well go for a marathon. It isn't like you have to go to work in a few minutes. Take your time. Enjoy yourselves. Make a memory to last forever.

It is better if you are on top, first. He is just an older man. *(Don't tell him I said that!)* He doesn't have a lot of strength in reserve, not any more. What strength he does have you want to save for round two. If he has had a bit of trouble keeping it up in the past, put a pillow under his hips before you mount him. This aids amazingly in his sexual response. Don't let him put his head on a pillow. You want his penis to be the highest part of his body.

Don't slide it in and get to it. Sit on top of him and rub your clitoris down the length of his penis. He will love it. He will get the feeling that you are using his body to get yourself off, an idea that men, as screwed up as we are, totally love. *(Natasha taught me that!)* Slide him inside when you can't take it anymore. Don't put your hands on the bed. Put them on his chest; put them on his nipples. If you feel him losing some of his hardness twist and pinch his nipples, both at the same time if possible. When you feel yourself almost ready to come, reach down and bite one of his nipples, hard. Don't worry; you aren't going to hurt him. His areole is made of the same tough skin as yours. If babies can bite, so can you! If you have done your foreplay properly, he will enlarge tremendously when you sink your teeth into him and you will come like you never have before. He will also. Don't allow him to pull out. You are in charge, you are on top. If you use your vaginal wall muscles to tighten around him, the blood won't be able to escape from his penis as you orgasm over and over again. Most women can orgasm *at least* six times about five minutes apart if you can keep your guy's penis hard. He won't care. If you did your foreplay correctly, he will be laying there with a smile on his face and his eyes dilated in pleasure. He will be smiling at you getting off over and over again. He won't be jealous. He will think he is a great lover. Men are weird. Actually, you did all the work. You deserve the pleasure!

Eventually it will be over. He will shrink and slip out, no matter what you do. Now is the time to lie in each other's arms and maybe even take a wee nap. If you can, reach down and hold his penis in your hand. You don't want it to get cold and after all your foreplay you don't want him to think he is going to get off that easy!

Oral sex is not good for foreplay. It really isn't. Maybe when you were both younger it was great. You know, when you were trying to get to all the bases in turn. When your guy is over 60+ it isn't. It is good for afterplay, however. After you wake from your nap, twist around and put his penis in your mouth. I know, yuck. Get past it, girl. We are talking about a night of love that you will remember for the rest of your life. Take him into your mouth. You will be able to deep throat him; to put him entirely into your mouth as he is so small. Don't tire yourself out bobbing your head up and down. It is just so much wasted effort. Instead, run your tongue over his length *(maybe just a couple of inches, now)* over and over again. It isn't difficult as he is still so small. If he wants to play with you, let him. You will still be very relaxed down there and if he is adventurous, he might even be able to find your clitoris! In a surprisingly short time he will start to get hard. The dorsal side of the penis, the top side, has all the nerve endings. If you can, massage that side with your tongue. If you want to play rough, be rough with the ventral side. A man's penis, when erect, is roughly triangular in shape. The base side of the triangle, next to the stomach, is the side with all the nerve endings.

While we are on the subject, giving a man a hand job *(as it is known in the vernacular)* is a lost art. Here is how to do it. I'm not telling you that you have been doing it wrong, I know your guy likes it the way you do it, I am telling you how to do it better, so much better that it will blow his brain! If your man still has his foreskin, you are luck. You can grab hold of it any which way and start pumping flesh. If he has been cut, like so many of us older men, you have to be more careful. Put your hand on the apex of his penis' triangle first, pull the skin down and then and only then close your hand around the rest of his penis. The base of his penis triangle is full of nerve endings and if it is stretched more than the apex, it hurts.

There is a better way. Lubricate your hands and his penis well, and then slide one hand down the length of his penis, pinkie first. As long as you are well lubricated you won't hurt the base of his penis. As soon as your hands' thumb has cleared the tip of his penis, move your other hand down his penis in the same way. As soon as that hand is almost down, release your first hand and have it follow the first hand in an endless rotation. This is far easier and less athletic for you and will really blow his little brain wide open and both of his heads!

Linda Lovelace did a lot of harm to women in her movie, Deep Throat. Guys get off when you do deep throat them because they think they are supposed to. Men are complicated! Far better is when your man gets hard is to go down on him and put his penis into your mouth, the tip of it touching the top of your mouth. Run your tongue up the top of your mouth right now. There is a little hollow spot at the top. It kind of tickles when your tongue touches it, doesn't it? *(This is the area adepts push the tips of their tongues into when doing difficult yoga exercises. It connects the body to the brain using yet another pathway.)* When you go down on him push the tip of his penis into this spot and lick his spot between the head and the shaft with your tongue. He might start out thinking, "Hey, Linda Lovelace didn't do it this way!" But give it a few minutes and he will change his mind about who his favorite movie star is! Once he gets used to it, he will orgasm in record time this way. An advantage is that it won't tire you out. There is lots of loving yet to come!

In between a man's testicles and his anus is an area called the perineum. This is a very interesting erogenous zone. There is a ridge containing a nerve sheath that runs between the penis and the anus, on either side of this ridge, halfway between, are two fairly circular holes about an inch apart that the testicles originally descended from during puberty. These holes allow a woman in the know to access the entire length of a man's penis. The penis doesn't start at the skin. It is rooted to the pelvic arch deep within a man's hips. Almost half of his penis is inside his body! Sliding her fingers into these holes allows a lover to stroke the lower internal half of a penis. It isn't easy however. After the testicles drop, the holes they dropped from start to fill in with a fat like substance. So what you do is slide your fingers along between the anus and scrotum feeling for the holes. They will just be little dimples at first. When you find them, gently, slowly push your fingers in. Long nails are a minus here. The fat like substance will resist, but with constant, consistent pressure it will give way. It might take a few days of trials before you are able to sink your fingers in all the way to the second knuckle. Inside the stiff penis is obvious. Stroke on either side of the shaft with your fingers as you tend to the outer part with your other hand or mouth. This is an advanced technique but one well worth exploring. Talk about a way to get a man hard!

By now he will be fully erect *(Very)* and ready to go. It is his turn. Let him take you doggie style. Lots of women don't like this position both because they feel it is degrading and because they don't get enough clitoral stimulation. *(Wait. Finish the paragraph. Really! You owe it to yourself.)* Men love the doggie position because it gives them a feeling of power and it is easier for them physically as they can use their hands as well as their hips to thrust into you. Because of the way a woman's body is constructed, in this position her vagina feels much tighter to a man. The main problem happens when the man is getting ready to come; he slows down, enjoying each thrust, savoring it, just when the woman wants him to be pounding into her. What a girl should be doing is to reach between her legs and find his scrotum. It will be clenched up tight to his body by now. Grab a little bit of skin and pull. Don't grab his balls, just the skin. Slowly the skin will ease away from his testicles and you will be able to get a good, firm hold on it. Now, take over the rhythm. Pull his scrotum; pull him into you as hard or tender and as fast or slow as you want. I guarantee that he will follow your lead. After all, you have him by the short and curlys! Even if he is missing your clitoris, pound him into your bottom and vagina and the resulting shock will transfer over to your clitoris and you will come in shocking waves! Don't forget to breathe!

Take a little nap again. It isn't over yet! When you both wake up, run your fingernails up his back all the way from his butt to his neck if you can. Sink your nails into his skin after a few minutes. He won't mind. He will get an erection much faster this time. The second time takes the longest for him to get hard. If he isn't that stiff, hold the head of his penis between the base of your thumb and forefinger, pull up a bit, and start tapping his penis with the forefinger's tip on the triangle's point, the part away from his stomach. Tap lightly from just below the penis's head to between his balls. When he gets used to it, tap harder. It won't hurt him between the balls as long as you don't make a mistake and hit his testicles instead. Especially don't hit them with a glancing blow. That hurts the worse. While you are busy playing with him, let him do what he wants. He has earned it. If he wants to play between your legs, let him. It takes 60 to 90 minutes for the next batch of testosterone to arrive. There is no hurry. If he is taking his time getting hard, spend the time educating him. Teach his how to make you squirt.

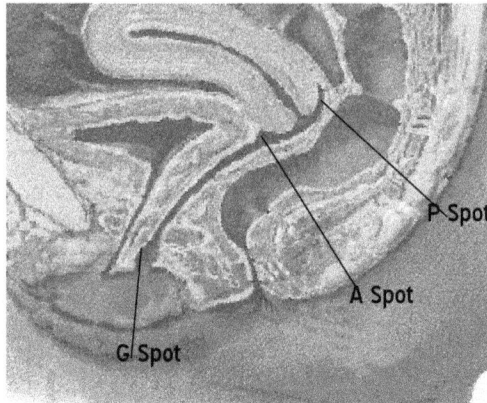

Inner Erogenous Zones
In the Female

Anni

I met Anni in a small island in Indonesia. I saw her first windowing rice. This is when you pour a large bowl of field rice held at breast height down onto a woven rug while standing in the trade winds. The wind blows the chaff away downwind while the heavier rice falls straight down. She looked so beautiful, so unobtainable. I was in my early twenties so I didn't see anything wrong with staring and staring and staring.

Something must have clicked between us as late that night I heard a knocking on my hull. It was a very naked Anni! She had left her clothes on the beach. What a night we had! It was never to be repeated as I was cruising Indonesia without a cruising permit and the next morning a military boat circled the island, so I sped off broken hearted.

Anni was saving herself for her eventual husband. She wanted to be a virgin for him. She wanted me to enter her through her anus. I never knew women could orgasm that way, but boy she did! My god! Over and over and over. She kept me inside her somehow and kept on coming and coming. It must have lasted an hour!

The only thing I have to say is some Indonesian guy got himself one hell of a wife!

Chapter Four
Making Love
Part Two

A squirting orgasm is the most powerful orgasm a woman can have. It isn't easy to do, but practice makes perfect. Younger men usually don't have the patience. They get bored and drill you instead out of frustration. A lover over 60 isn't in so much of a hurry. Theoretically it isn't difficult. You will have to give your man a lot of verbal clues. You can't be shy. If you are, hope for the best.

The clitoris is a long shaft, much like the penis, when excited. The other end of the clitoris is what has been called the G spot. *(G as the guy who first described it first was named Grafenberg. You would have thought it would have been a Frenchman, wouldn't you?)* It is a slightly roughened area inside the vagina more or less behind the clitoris. To the exploring finger it feels like the skin of a walnut. *(Kind of)* Once you are excited enough *(the G spot hides normally behind a fold of skin)* for him to find it; have him lightly tap it with a pad of a finger. It isn't difficult; it is only a couple of inches inside with a hook towards the belly. Once the surrounding flesh of the vagina starts to retract, to open the vagina slightly, have him curl his finger and make a come here motion over and over again, maybe twice a heartbeat. You will start to get seriously turned on now. If he is too busy to do it, play with your clitoris yourself. As you get even more excited, have him put two fingers in and shove them in and out, ramming into your G spot. Make sure, beforehand, that he has short, clean nails. If he has rough hands or hang nails, have him wear a rubber glove or condom on them, your vagina will thank you in the morning. You will get more and more excited. Don't let him stop. Don't let him slow down. Have him suck one of your nipples into his mouth, actually just into his lips. When you get more and more excited it is ok for him to nibble slightly. *(Most women who have breast fed babies are very protective of their nipples, but as long as he goes slow, it will be alright.)* Before you know it you will have a nipple stand. This is when your nipple elongates and stiffens to an inch to an inch and a half. Most women can orgasm from just a nipple stand. Back to your G-spot. You will suddenly feel that you have to pee. Ignore it. You don't. During sex a valve closes the bladder off. You can't pee. Suddenly you will start to come. You will scream. You will scream loud enough to wake the neighbors. You will squirt out a substance very like a seminal fluid out of your vagina. A lot of it. Seemingly gallons. You will drench your guy if he is in the firing range. You will scream every molecule of air out of your lungs in incredible joy.

Beforehand instruct him to let you sleep when you are finished. You will be able to do little else. Have him organize a couple of glasses of water for when you wake. You will be very thirsty. And very, very happy! The distance record for a squirt is ten feet. You might want to use your old sheets or do it outside!

It isn't urine that you are squirting out. It is very much like the seminal fluid that comes out of a man's prostate. In women it comes out of the paraurethral glands. There are at least 4 of them. Some girls have 6. These are the glands that keep your vagina lubricated during sex. If you have reached the age where you are starting to need more and more lubricant, it will be interesting to note that squirting seems to wake these glands back up. Bet you didn't know that!

When you awaken, his body will be loaded with testosterone again. Time for fun and games! It is his turn now. It should be after he made you squirt. He might want to be on top but seeing as how he is over 60, you might want him to do it side by side. Allow him to do it. He earned the right. However, lie on your back when he is on his side. Organize yourself so that you raise one leg and pull his upper leg over on top of your stomach. As he starts pumping, make sure his upper leg is rubbing your clitoris' hood area. It works better if his leg only touches going down towards your feet. He is actually massaging your K spot but don't tell him. He isn't capable of thinking right now. Keep your hands on his leg and guide him. *(More on the K spot later!)* Reach over and play with his nipples to make sure he doesn't run out of testosterone. When you are almost ready, dig a nail into his nipple and he will come in waves of passion, pulling you into orgasm along with him. *(That part was from Natasha!)* Don't dig in a nail and leave it there. Dig it in just for a second. That is all that is needed. Maybe another nudge five seconds later, a bit of rubbing and twisting in between.

Simultaneous orgasms should never be a rare thing. It is so much better when you come together; not doing so is kind of lame. It isn't hard to do. Once you know your partner's signs, it is fairly easy to do. For the guy, he can feel the girl's vagina start to pulsate pulling his penis deeper in; for the girl she can feel the guy's penis's head engorge to block the way for any sperm that might want to swim the other way. Just feeling your partner's excitement often brings you to orgasm itself. It is great having a lover over 60 years of age. He has the time and the patience to do a good job of loving you.

Life size photo of the G spot in a woman's vagina.

Virginia

I met Virginia in the Seychelles on the island of Praslin. She was a Kiwi girl from New Zealand off of another boat. She was boatwatching while her captain was away on business. She was dressing the boat up tying decorative knots all over the place.

Virginia taught me about the joys of bondage. At least half of it. She liked to tie me up and have her way however she wanted it. I wasn't allowed to tie her up. Not that I cared. She was beautiful, she was sexy and I had been at sea for a long time!

She liked to blindfold me and then tickle various parts of my body until I was as hard as a rock. She was the first to drop hot wax on my body from a living candle, making occult designs. I wondered sometimes if she might have been a witch in a previous incarnation!

She liked to be in control. I didn't mind. I was having the experience of a life time! As she made love on top, she slid her body towards my feet to drag her clitoris against the base of my penis's triangle. The base has little ridges along its length. It was great for both of us!

After a month, I left her and the Seychelles, very happy to be out at sea again. I later realized that her captain didn't have business back in New Zealand, he just needed a break!

Chapter Five
Making Love
Part Three

You would think that it will take him a long time to recover after all the loving you have been giving him. It doesn't though. He is doing it so often; his body is flooded with testosterone. But he is an older man. You don't want to give him a heart attack. Time to cool things down again. Might as well give him another lesson while he is resting. Your G spot most likely will be fairly sore after squirting, but it isn't the only spot in your vagina. You actually can obtain a more dependable orgasm with the A spot.

The A spot *(Anterior Fornix Erogenous Zone, if you are cramming for the test)* is between the outer edge on your cervix and the vaginal wall on your belly side. Guide his hand in. Believe me he will love it. Just tell him you are going to teach him a magic spot on a woman's body that will make her fall in love with him. It is his dream from High School coming true after all! The Cervix hides when you are not turned on. Tell him that and make him work at it! Actually with all the sex you have been getting you probably are permanently turned on anyway!

If your cervix is hiding have him play with your U spot to get yourself more excited. *(Urethral Opening Erogenous Zone)*. It is a twin area on each side of your urethral opening, where you pee out of. Don't let him touch it with his fingers. He will be too rough. No matter how soft his fingers, he will be too rough. Make him use his tongue. If he can, have him make a u shape with his tongue and touch you with that, if not then a flick on each side over and over with the tip of his tongue will do the trick. You can orgasm this way but hold out for the A spot! It is so much better! If his tongue is getting tired, switch him over to your k spot. *(I don't know the right name, but just to be confusing, there are two K zones! The other is the Kundalini Erogenous Zone which lies on the perineum between the anus and the bottom of the vagina. This spot is fine when you are young but after child birth, especially after an episiotomy, it is history. Because we are all a bit overaged here and the kids have hopefully fled the nest, it is has been turned off. Are you taking notes?)* The k spot is just above your clitoris on the apex of the clitoral hood outside of your vagina. Again a tongue is much better than a finger. You can definitely orgasm with this site, as the pressure of his tongue will also be pushing against your clitoris, hidden below, with its 8000 nerve endings. *(The clitoris has more nerve endings than an equal size area of the human brain. Who says God isn't a woman?)* If your labia are small, it might be that your k spot gets too much stimulation from your panties and has turned itself off. You either have to live with them turned off or stop wearing panties! Longer hair down there does help with keeping your k spots active. *(With all the letters in the alphabet, you would think they wouldn't have to use the same one twice, wouldn't you?)*

When you are ready, let him slide a finger inside of you. He will have to go deep. He will have to sink his longest finger into you and maybe a bit of his hand. He will feel the cervix sticking out into the middle of your vagina. It has a thin shaft and blossoms out into a flower arrangement at the end. The A spot is between the edge of the flower and the vaginal wall on your belly side, that is where you want him to stroke. *(The spot is actually on the wall but he will never find it if he doesn't have the cervix to guide him. It feels like a little dimple and is rougher than the surrounding wall.)* Teach him that a light steady stroke is best. Often it is better to tell him to rub your cervix. That will make sure he is gentle with your A spot. If you twirl your finger around the tuft of hair on the nape of his neck and slightly tug each time you want him to stroke, things will go fine. It won't take long. Most women come in less than 60 seconds with an A spot orgasm. *(Size does make a difference. If your man's penis is long enough to reach your A spot, you are a lucky girl! Actually, at rest, your vagina is only 4 inches long. However when excited the length can easily double!)* When you do orgasm, your vagina will squeeze his finger (s) very painfully. Tell him to be a man. Make him keep his fingers in there and keep massaging that spot. Tell him if he does, he will be in for the ride of his life! Sometimes, if you masturbate a lot, your clitoris will harden with excess collagen and you will lose most of the feeling in it. If this happens to you, go on a diet of A spot orgasms. The A spot is the epicenter of your orgasms and after a week or so of daily A spot orgasms your clitoris will return from the dead; like a phoenix reborn in the flames!

He is going to be ready again. When a girl orgasms, she releases oxytocin in her breath. Kiss him when you are finished your six or so mini orgasms. After your orgasm (s), kiss him and breathe lightly into his mouth and puff ever so lightly in to his nose. You will be surprised at the results!

Let him be on top now. He has earned it. If he is like most men, he will just jump on and start pumping away. In and out like a pile driver. Well, an old wheezing, over used pile driver. Before he dies from a coronary, you had better give him some lessons. Be sweet, be kind. He thinks he is doing it right. If you destroy his self-esteem, he will be worthless in the sack.

Put your hands on his butt cheeks to guide and encourage him. What you want him to do is raise up his hips and thrust down, *(actually he is doing that part just fine)*, then you want him to pivot his hips forward when he is all the way in and give a little final push. The pivot is to push your labia up exposing your clitoris and the last push is to touch your little nub of joy. This won't work if either of you have long pubic hair. Keep it trimmed, not scratchy, but not old man of the mountain, either! *(He will love you to trim it for him. If he starts to get frisky, remind him pointedly, that you have a sharp pair of shears right next to his goodies!)* This is an athletic position for him at his age so if he starts tire and to lose his hardness, slip a finger between his cheeks and touch his anus. The anus has a plethora of nerve endings on the outside and even more just inside. I think God must have been a jokester when he created us as touching his anus also releases testosterone into his blood stream. More that that, it has a direct nerve connecting it to the penis, just like the nipples do, this swells his penis. The anus used to be called the 'get it over with button' as he will come within seconds after you touch him there.

(A warning here. In case you have ever wondered, there is a way to tell if a man has leadings towards being a homosexual. All men get

harder when their anus is touched. However, if you push a penis size object into his colon he will lose his erection if he is inherently a heterosexual, or get even harder if he is homosexual or bisexual. If he does get harder, don't say anything to him. He probably doesn't know. Just because he has leanings doesn't mean he is or ever will be. Loose lips sink ships, or in this case, ruin your sex life. By the way, just because he is less hard, doesn't mean he can't come. Use your hand with a very light touch and he will come in average time. Isn't the male body strange? Men are complicated. The majority of the human race is bisexual. Most of us don't follow those tendencies as we develop our sexual orientation early in life and never change. Every human has two sexual responses hard wired into the brain. One 'mounting', masculine, and two 'mounted' feminine. Each behavior can be activated by hormones injected into the blood system in lower animals. In humans it is more complicated as the brain can override any behavior it thinks is inappropriate. Maybe it isn't just men that are complicated!)

As long as we are talking about the anus, well, let's talk about it. It is a great love making area but there are some rules. The first thing is cleanliness. Always douche before getting anywhere near the anus and colon. There are many douches available in all pharmacies. It is worth it. Infections are a terrible thing and, well, they ruin your sex life. There, that is out of the way. Now we can have fun! Oh, wait. A man should always wear a condom when entering 'thru the back door' as they so colorfully phrase it, especially if he intends to penetrate the vagina later. Ok. Phew! Back to the fun stuff! Thank goodness!

A woman has a P spot deep in her vagina. *(Posterior Fornix Erogenous Zone)* It is too deep for all but the longest endowed males too reach and far too deep for fingers no matter how you might twist and turn. However, it can be easily reached through the anus. The wall that separates the vagina and the colon is very thin; thrusts can easily be felt in the other department as one might say. The P spot area is at the base of the cervix and the vagina on the wall separating the vagina and the colon. From the anus side the P spot is only 5 inches or so inside, easily reached by almost all penises.

Before you let him enter your 'backdoor', he has to earn it first. Have him massage your anus with plenty of lubricant. Just on the outside at first, massage it until the anus will actually seem to pull his finger inside. An inch or so inside the anus is a circle of muscle called the sphincter, which job is to keep the feces inside and the rest of the world outside until you are ready to defecate. He can push all he wants against this muscle and he won't get anywhere, unless he is willing to hurt you. Instead, have him stick his smallest finger inside and run it around the inside lip of the sphincter muscle. This will release the muscle and allow his penis to enter. Once your sphincter has released, have him condomed up and lubricated, if he waits too long the sphincter will seal up again! The best way for his penis to rub your P spot is for you to sit on top of him and face him. Don't slide back towards his legs; you want his penis to be jutting forward. As his head starts to swell, *(The penis' head, that is! Not that the other won't be!)* It will start rubbing against the P spot. Don't be surprised if you squirt a little here too! It is a very strong orgasm. Don't let the blood escape from his penis. Your sphincter is very strong. It can trap his penis inside of you. Enjoy all the mini orgasms that will follow. Every time someone establishes a record for the number of orgasms for the P spot, the week following someone else breaks it. I believe the record is now over 62 and she only stopped then as the poor thing fell asleep, exhausted!

Men seem to have this fixation of having anal sex in the 'doggie' position. That doesn't work for the ladies. It misses the P spot entirely. Other than the above, better is lying on your stomach and have him on top with a pillow under your hips. *(Thailand sells triangular pillows available in most import stores that are great for anal sex. Put the point of the triangle down on the bed and your back on the base of the triangle. This way he can rock you back and forth easily and gently.)* Next best is him in a semi prone sitting position and you in control, your back facing him. Men love the sight of a woman's back. It is one of the most beautiful parts of a woman's body. Don't be embarrassed by letting him enjoy it! Some women have an enlarged P spot and can orgasm whenever, however, they are entered anally. Lucky girls.

A man doesn't have any of these 'spots', worse the luck; however he does have a prostate gland. The prostate lies just inside the anus, go past the sphincter muscle, yes he has one too, and make a hard turn towards the penis. It feels to the exploratory finger like a walnut shell.

Sexually inactive men have to be 'milked.' A doctor *(actually a nurse)* sticks her gloved finger in a man's anus, strokes the prostate and releases volumes of seminal fluid through the penis that the prostate has been busy storing up, just in case. Left too long this seminal fluid turns toxic and harms the prostate causing all kinds of trouble. Sexually active men don't have to worry about this.

If you really want to give your man an experience he will never forget, stick your gloved finger in his douched anus and stroke his prostate with a gentle circular motion. It will feel to him like your finger is inside his penis. *(Men have a really weird nervous system!)* For added fun, sit on top of him, back towards his face, him inside of you, while you stroke his prostate. It is about the strongest orgasm a man can have and while it is nothing compared to a squirting orgasm; guys have to accept what they can get! He should swell up when you stroke his prostate, if not be sure to sit on him first and clamp down on him so he doesn't lose his erection.

A woman has a perineum also. It is also an erogenous zone, at least until she has a baby. Usually the perineum is sliced open during childbirth for a faster, less dangerous birth. Sometimes the doctor is more careful and he won't slice the nerve between your vagina and your anus. If he didn't, have your man rub a forefinger along the nerve sheath between the two while rubbing your clitoris. Don't do this when people are around. They will think he is hurting you, so loudly you will be screaming! If your clitoris is not erect when you are making love, *(no clitoral erection, no orgasm)* have your man push against your perineum while playing with your clitoris gently. He should push about as hard as pushing against jello but not so hard that his finger pushes into the jello. This is a trigger point of a women's body. It sends a surge of blood into the clitoris and g spot making them both ready for love after just a minute or two of contact.

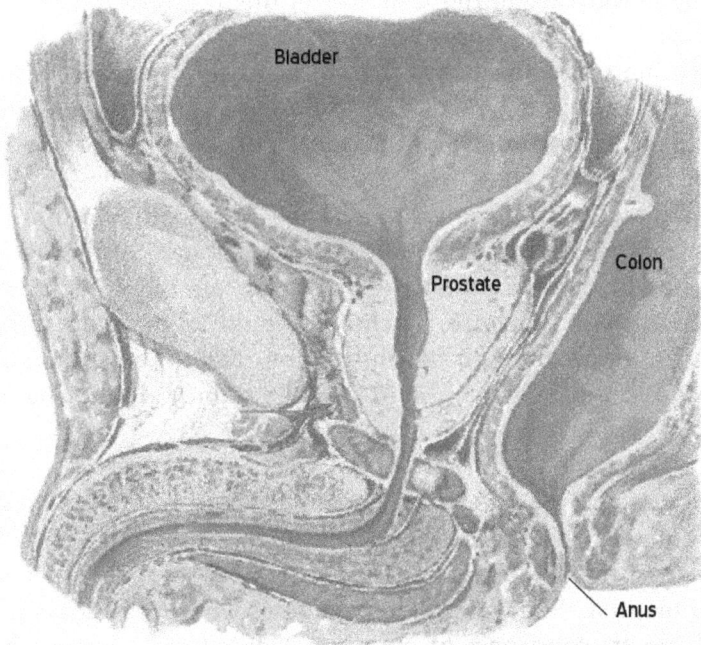

Inner Erogenous Zone
In the Male

Sally

I met Sally in Mayotte in the Comores in the Western Indian. She was an American Peace Corps worker who had been on island a bit too long. She loved the island, but she had tired of the constant barrage of Frenchmen trying to date her. She needed a bit of a recess, a break from land. Sometimes it is a blessing to have a boat!

Sally grew up in Indiana somewhere. The Peace Corps was her first time she saw the ocean and another country. But it wasn't the first time she had been with a man. Realize that I am not complaining! We sailed around Mayotte, anchoring in little beautiful coves, making love on abandoned beaches. One beautiful windless day, she decided to educate me. Mind you, she didn't tell me what she was going to do, first.

While we were 69'ing, she stuck her fingers into the twin holes of my perineum. With her other hand, she stuck a finger into my colon and massaged my prostate. Imagine my shock! At least she could have told me first. She was sucking my penis while her fingers were inside of me stroking part of my penis I didn't even know I had, while her finger in my colon felt like it was inside my penis, vibrating! What a revelation!

I have always intended to visit Indiana. It must be a very sexy place. Either that or she didn't escape the attention of all of those educating Frenchmen!

Chapter Six
After Sex

Making love is the most wonderful thing that two people can do for each other. It bonds them together into a single unit, yes, but more importantly, after sex is over, if they lay together, defenses down, multiple versions of themselves cast aside to bare their true selves, you can truly get to know your partner. Your real partner. After sex is over, especially after a marathon love session has expired, you both will lie there exhausted, yes, but also without pretense. There is no need for talking. Your souls, your spirits are conversing without such a new flung device like conversation. *(Actually, cave men did grunt a lot. I guess that could be construed as conversation!)* Don't go rushing off after sex to take a shower or to check on the grandkids. If the phone rings, let it ring. Dare each other, if you must, to not be the first to break such a magical moment. Hold each other close. A kiss now, after, is the most enduring kiss of all. Instead of being full of passion and desire, it is full of acceptance, love and understanding. I truly believe that the divorce rate could be easily halved if people would just cuddle and kiss each other after making love.

Don't talk after making love, not about what you just did. What is there to talk about? Your bodies have just said it all. Smile at each other, gaze kindly into each other's eyes, inhale each other's breaths. Cuddle as if you are never going to let the other go. Be one with each other. The feeling of oneness will fade in time. In fifteen minutes, you will be thinking about what to have for dinner, he will be thinking when the ball game will be on the idiot box. It is too bad this moment is so short. Be sure to enjoy it when you can. Treasure it.

After sex is when oral, well, not sex, but touching reaches its highest expression. Lick him clean or if you are factitious, have a soft cloth handy to clean him with. Be kind, those orgasms gave you enormous pleasure. Take care of that penis! Allow him to try to clean you if he wants before you take over the job. Men seem to think they are supposed to lick you clean afterwards. Let them down easy. You don't want to break their little hearts. Let him try to wipe you with a cloth. After, take a shower together. If he doesn't want to kiss, if he has obtained what he wanted, snuggle into him, your head on his shoulder. Allow him to feel how soft and compliant your body is. Rub your hand over him. Let him know how much you love him. If he has a chubby tummy, as so many 60+ men do, rub your hand over that too, let him know that you love all of him, every part. Even if he is resistant at first to your cuddling after sex, keep it up. He will come around eventually.

As you do the chores your life might demand, do them together after sex. While you do them, glide a hand over his shoulders. Encourage him to run his hand over your behind. Sex is over, love isn't. Love is just getting started. What you do after sex determines how much your love will develop. If you jump out of bed and rush off to your various occupations, there is little hope for your love to get any stronger than it already is. It might even degrade. Don't let it. Screw his brains out and then love him with every molecule in your body. That is the recipe of a happy marriage.

As soon as you have finished recovering from making love, start building the tension for the next time. Don't come on too strong at first. After all, if you did all of the above, you probably are having trouble even walking. *(Whatever you do, don't put on jeans. The agony!)* You are having trouble walking in any thing short of a hobble! When you talk, be sure to call him Stud or Lover. Try to keep away from Honey and Sweetheart. I know that is what you want him to call you, but if you want even greater sex next time, start getting him ready. It isn't like he is a 20 something. He is over 60 and things take longer to get started. Might as well plant the thought in his brain. Right now, he is feeling a bit drained and very tired. Don't accept that. The more you make love, the more you can and the longer you can. If he tries to make some moves on you right now, let him down easy. He doesn't have enough testosterone in his veins to make it worth while. Tell him how sore you are. Tell him you will be better tomorrow. Tell him you will be better than ever tomorrow and tomorrow you will be raring to go. Don't let making love fall into a once a month affair or even once a week event. With practice, the two of you can be doing some kind of loving well into your 90's. Plus the longer you make love, the longer you will live. A hidden secret of hospitals and retirement homes is people die of boredom. Their quality of life is so low; they feel they might as well be dead. Don't let that happen to the two of you. Grasp life with both hands and enjoy the hell out of it. The very best part of your life can be sexual love. Why not make it so? You can. The more you make love, the more you will want to. Do it every day that you can!

Remember, sex starts in the brain. The brain has to release all those hormones to get things going. The brain has to fire those nerves leading down to the penis. Keep putting ideas in his head. Let him know you want him. Let him know you desire him. Let him know you can't live without his loving. Ok. That last was a bit over the top. But you get the idea. It's all about hormones!

Janie

I met Janie in Hawaii. She was mostly Hawaiian with a lot of Spanish mixed in somehow. She was a wonderful girl. I fell deeply in love with her. I would have married her in a heartbeat if she wasn't afraid of the water.

Janie taught me over the two years we were together that sex wasn't good if you didn't love each other. One night stands were fine but they were little more than mutual masturbation.

Janie taught me that there was just as much love in making a meal together as giving a kiss, as much love in turning down the covers of a bed as giving a guy oral sex.

Janie was a fun girl. She liked to explore and she wasn't shy at all. If I mentioned something we might try sexually, even in passing, she tore off her clothes and wanted to try it right then. It didn't matter if we were in a store; she pushed me into a closet and went for it. There wasn't anything she wouldn't try.

But behind it all, she only acted so because she was head over heels in love with me and I with her. Sex is so much better when you are in love. Maybe that is why they call it making love, not making sex?

The call of the sea was too strong in my heart and eventually I left my Janie. On that day, I wept. Late at night, when I can't sleep, I still remember her with incredible fondness.

Chapter Seven
Sexual Foods

Diet plays an important part of love making. We all know about it. Oysters. Right? Red meat, maybe not. What is really important is garlic. Garlic is easy. Put it in every meal you can. Did you ever wonder why Italian men have such a reputation as wonderful lovers? Plenty of raw garlic! Try to feed your man at least a clove a day. He won't know if you disguise it! What the garlic does, especially when raw, is increases the flexibility of the arteries and veins leading to the penis. This allows more blood to get to his penis allowing it to get much larger! Larger is definitely good! His breath won't smell so bad if you eat some too!

Ginger is a natural aphrodisiac for women. Really! It has to be fresh and peeled. Rub it on your labia and if you are very brave, your clitoris! The affect is astounding! The poor man won't know what hit him when you turn into this sex crazed woman! Ginger doesn't work as well for him. Gay men insert a peeled finger of garlic into their anus. I tried it when researching for this book but never got much of a charge out of it, but maybe that is just me. Do you have to be gay?

Don't worry too much about calories. If you keep up this sexual appetite you have developed, both of you will be thin, you svelte, him stud-like. If anyone wants to know what has changed your life, tell them, vitamins. It is an easy answer and is half way true. The idea of nutrition in today's world is to stuff everyone with hundreds of vitamins just in case they might need one. The human body produces all the vitamins it needs out of food except for vitamin C. Why doesn't the body produce vitamin C? You might want to watch the movie Jurassic Park again! I fantasize that we are an experiment developed by aliens and they designed us to require vitamin C as a way to kill us off if things got out of hand. What has this to do with Red Hot Males over Sixty? Sorry. Sorry. We writers love to get up on our little soap boxes and expound. Forgive Me!

Because our bodies require vitamin C make sure he gets enough of it. Forget and apple a day, an orange a day is what it should be! Without sufficient vitamin C he will not last long in bed. And we need him to be a sexual dynamo!

Magazines publish articles all about how this sex act or that will burn so many calories. They are missing the point. Losing weight is about increasing the metabolic rate, the speed your cells are reproducing. It is good to increase this rate. Cells that are damaged are reproduced and replaced faster, your skin will be gorgeous. Your hair will grow in leaps and bounds, might have to cut it more often, but most important, your sexual health will go into overdrive, so will your man's. Ever wonder why some people can eat as much as they want and never gain a pound? Try making love to one. They are little energizer bunnies! The more you make love, the faster your metabolic rate will increase. They are going to put your face on the cover of magazines if you follow all the directions in this book!

Avocados have long been called the fruit of the gods for good reason. They taste wonderful and they are a complete food. *(You can survive very happily on just avocados. They are the only fruit with serious amounts of protein! As well as all the vitamins, including C!)* Avocado oil for some reason goes straight to your paraurethral glands, making the need for lubricant not as necessary. Better sex through diet!

Red meat is always suggested as a pre-sex meal. It is not a good idea. Meat takes a long time to digest and uses a large amount of the bodies' blood supply to do so. We don't want to share. We want that blood to fuel our love making! Far better is a baked potato. Really! The lowly potato is a wonderful food for lowering high blood pressure. And we do want to lower our blood pressure. Actually what we really want to do is to relax the walls of the arteries and the veins around the heart to increase the blood flow to, well, all the body, but mostly the penis. Without enough blood, it will never be able to get to the rock hard, blue ball, state you desire!

We like to treat the ones we are attempting to seduce with special foods. Chocolate is high on the list. That is a good idea but make sure it is dark chocolate, not milk chocolate. Dark chocolate also increases the blood flow to the vagina. Girls need increased blood flow also. The more blood flow, the tighter the vagina will be! The best of all dark chocolate are nibs. This is part of the cocoa bean after it is picked from the tree. Nibs are uncooked, delicious, and can really turn on both sexes!

Grapes and red wine are also favorites. They both dilate the veins, capillaries and arteries allowing more blood flow into sexual areas and help to release any inhibitions we might have to new sexual explorations. Grapes are so much fun. You can feed each other; you can place them in interesting places and have your partner devour them one way or the other. They can be passed one to the other during a kiss, even! Grapes are fun! Even tongues need exercise!

Strawberries dipped in dark chocolate were made for sex. No way they weren't. They are so much fun to feed to each other. And good for you! A strawberry, dipped in chocolate, served with red wine is about as good for sex as you can get. Chocolate contains a molecule that mimics oxytocin in the brain. Eating it with wine speeds it on its way, and the strawberry makes it fun!

The inside of a fig looks like a vagina. Supposedly, if you take your time eating an opened fig in front of a woman, well, this one is an old wives tale. But it could be true! Walnuts are supposed to be a great sex food. They may well be. More importantly, the surface of a walnut feels to the finger just like the G spot in a woman's vagina! Have your man practice with one first! A walnut also feels like a man's prostate. Maybe both of you should practice and then devour!

Almonds are great for sex as are cayenne pepper and sweet basil but the master is zinc. Modern men are woefully deficient in zinc. An easy way to tell, is if your man grows long eyebrows or has excessive amounts of sleep in his eyes in the morning, he is zinc deficient. Zinc is very important in testosterone production. Go down to the Dollar Store and buy him a bottle of tablets. Keep score in a secret code on your calendar. I bet your orgasms will go up after he is popping zinc! Shellfish is the best natural source of zinc. On the other hand, if he is a walking man, ever time he goes by one of those supports for telephone poles, have him run a wet finger along the wire and then tell him to lick his finger. They are coated with almost pure zinc! The hell with germs. We are talking about getting laid, here!

Aniseed has been used for millennia as a supplement for sex. Plato started it and recommended its use for warriors in order to create more citizens soldiers to replace those lost in battle. Wait a minute. Does that also mean they take orders better? Wait. Listen. Girls, this could be interesting!

Bananas are a wonderful food to eat before sex. I know your mother told you not to play with your food, but I bet she would make an exception for bananas. If you get a banana before it gets too ripe, it makes a wonderful dildo, one that you can insert and then eat as you play with it! But we are getting into the next chapter! Be careful feeding your man bananas. They contain large amounts of estrogen, great for you, not for him; at least not if he wants to make love. Estrogen will reduce his testosterone levels making it difficult for him to become erect. He will be very understanding and loving, however! *(For more information, check out my book: How To Turn Your Woman into a Raving Nymphomaniac, For Men Only! Amazon.com/author/mike.riley)*

Eat well, love well. That about sums it up!

Sammie

I met Sammy in La Paz, Mexico when I was quite young. She was a full-blooded Aztec and liked to dance. This was during the disco era and she just had to go dancing every night. However, she couldn't go if she didn't have a guy to escort her in front of all her girl acquaintances. It was either an Aztec Pride thing or she was just acting like a girl.

I didn't mind. I loved to dance as well and Sammie made it worth my while to escort her. She loved to go down on me as the phrase goes. She was good at it. Really good. Many men get off as soon as female lips surround their penises. Not me. I have always been difficult. I never got off with oral sex. No problem with pubic sex. I loved it. I just had a problem with oral sex.

Sammie didn't. Have a problem, that is. Her desire, her passion to devour my penis was so overwhelming that I was pulled into her world and came in waves and waves of mind blowing, life altering sex. Many of the things she did down there have been added to this book. No wonder the Aztec Nation was defeated by Cortez. Their men were drained from so much sex!

Sammie and I stayed together for a long time. Eventually, she fell in love with a Mexican guy and married him. That guy must have spent the rest of his life in unbelievable happiness!

Chapter Eight
Marital Aids

No matter how hard we try, sometimes the hormones just aren't there. Maybe we are just too old. We need something more to tantalize the brain into releasing more of them into our bloodstream. Sometimes 'toys' can help quite well, it all depends on your own personal 'weirdness.' That is a strange word, isn't it? We all are weird if we judge ourselves by society's stated standards. Some of us laugh too loud, drink too much, stay up to all hours of the night. Some of us really like having our nipples touched or our clitorises fondled. Some of us like it hard, strong and heavy; others sweet, nice and gentle. It all comes down to what your brain gets off on. Don't judge. What happens in the privacy of your bedroom is for the two of you alone to know. If it turns you on, go for it. And we are all weird in one way or the other. Really! All of us! Especially the ones who say they aren't! They are the weirdest of us all! They are in denial! Anyway, it only feels kinky the first time!

There are a number of mechanical devices that turn on a woman, number one of these is a convertible Corvette. That is not a joke! However, the dildo is the most famous of marital aids. No, you don't have to go to the store and buy one in front of all those people. You can make your own by putting water into a condom that is contained inside of a paper towel roll and freezing it. Just be sure to lubricate it before touching any soft, moist tissues. You don't want it sticking to something down there like a tongue stuck to a stop sign pole in the snow! Another is a peeled cucumber or carrot! There are endless varieties of dildos for sale on the internet and at adult stores. The rabbit variety, popularized on the TV show, 'Sex in the City' is by far the most purchased. It vibrates at one speed inside the vagina and at another with little rabbit ears touching the clitoris. Women can orgasm dependably within 30 seconds. Amazing!

Even though dildos can stretch you out a bit, if your man is having trouble getting erect no matter what you try, let him please you with a dildo. Don't hold back your emotions. Let him know he is pleasing you, verbally and by your body writhing under his touch. Chances are once he gets you off with the dildo he will be so rock hard, you will be in for an encore. If nothing else happens, let him know that you like his equipment much better than some artificial device and cuddle with him. *(See Chapter Six)* In Thailand, they make a triangular pillow, triangular in cross section, that is a marvelous sexual aid for the 60+ man. It is available in most import houses, like Pier 21. Most people believe it is a pillow for leaning against. Nothing could be further from the truth! It is used with an apex of the triangle on the bed and the girl's body resting on the flat part of the triangle. It is very easy to move her body forward and back, pivoting on the tip of the triangle if the man gets tired of pounding into her. If she is face up, holding hands makes it very easy to move together. Face down, he can stay still and rotate her back and forth. The man can be on the pillow, face up, and the girl can change the angle of attack, to use jet fighter terminology, to make sure her clitoris is getting maximum stimulation.

One of the most interesting toys is a simple blindfold. We humans are visual creatures. We have let our other senses atrophy, so determined are we to rely mostly on vision. It is a revelation to deny your lover the ability to see. Suddenly all your other senses are shouting to be heard or touched or smelt. To make such an experience even more interesting is to tie your guy to the bed and deny him the ability to touch. Now when you touch his nipple or his penis, he will sense it far more powerfully than before. Pause between touching. If he is waiting to be touched, waiting to hear, waiting to taste, his mind is going to come alive and release tremendous amounts of hormones. Always determine a safe word before you tie someone up. A safe word is something a person would never normally say, for example, "wooden teeth." A safe word means stop what you are doing and untie me. This allows the tied up person to yell and beg to his hearts content, knowing you won't take him seriously. Sometimes it is fun to scream out, "No. Don't. Please Don't." Or "You just wait till I get out of these ropes, girl, I am going to show you who is stronger!" If he really wanted to get out, he just had to say the safe word!

The world seems to be obsessed with S/M these days. Just because you are tying your partner up, doesn't mean you have to hurt them, even in play. Pleasure can be so intense that the tied up person doesn't know whether to say stop or more! One of the most interesting marital aids, and one I invented myself, *(Ahem, excuse me as I pat myself on the shoulder!)* is the auto electric car polisher. This is a fairly big machine that moves randomly and slowly and puts out some very deep vibrations through a thick and soft pad. It is perfect for massaging as long as you take it easy. Most men will ejaculate easily when it is applied to their penises. All women will orgasm when it is applied to their pubic bone. When the polisher is to the buttocks, the vibrations relax the anus and make anal sex much easier and for the novice much less painful.

If both of your weirdnesses allow, twist and pull nipples, the penis, and the clitoris; spank his bottom, sit on his face and make him eat you. The possibilities are endless. Behind it all is an attempt to tantalize the brain. Never forget that important fact. It all comes down to getting the brain to release hormones. A wonderful light bondage toy is an electrical toothbrush. If you use a soft bristle, it is wonderful on the clitoris. Use a harder bristle for nipples, penises and testicles. Hot sauce does wonders for a nipple, it is left to your imagination what it might do for your labia, and even I hesitate to think what it might feel like on a clitoris! For a guy a dab on his nipples or his anus will turn him into a raving madman! Eat a mint before 'going down on him'. He will scream in delight. Don't let him do the same to you. Sugar gives the labia a rash. Maybe a diet mint?

Marital Aids manufacturers seemingly have no limit to their imagination. There are toys that shock you, massage you, vibrate you, and hurt you. The thing to remember is it doesn't matter what is happening to our erogenous zones, doesn't matter what these toys are doing, if your brain likes it. We are trying to get the brain to release voluminous amounts of hormones to make sex even more interesting than it already is. No matter how these toys can tantalize a man's body, nothing is going to turn him on as much as the sweet breath of a passionate lady. Not that marital aids are wrong. Far from it. They are fun! But they are no substitute for the real thing.

Role-playing is a marital aid that I know little about so it is difficult to write about, for me. However, many couples quite enjoy role-playing whether it is playing Doctor or bondage or simply dressing up as someone new. Paul de Kruif in his book, 'The Male Hormone', describes how men when encountering a new woman have as much as a 50% spike in their testosterone level. There is obviously something to it. Interestingly, he goes on to describe that for 3 years after marrying, a man's testosterone lowers and a female's increases. This honeymoon effect makes a reduction in the differences in the happy couple and makes him less interested in other women and she less interested in other men. Alas, it doesn't last! Parenthood also has the same effect on hormones. Perhaps that is a recipe for a happy marriage. Have your first kid 2 years and 11 months after getting married! Whether role-playing has an equal effect has not been studied. Perhaps when Margaret kept trying to get Dennis the Menace to play house, she was smarter than we realized. She was trying to lower his testosterone level! When you dress up as a different woman, his little male id some how thinks that you are. A different woman, that is. Whether it is as a nurse, a doctor, a schoolteacher, a prostitute, a mother, the idea is to get his brain to release more hormones. Hormones are good!

Role-playing is about experiencing the thrill of what could happen tempered with the safety of knowing that it cannot. Many women enjoy light bondage to allow their minds to come to grips with the horror of the possibility of being raped while knowing in the back of their minds that they are perfectly safe. The touch of their man's hands on her in this situation, floods her body with Oxytocin as her body protects her from the pain of what her mind is sure is going to occur. Rape is such a vicious crime because of the way a female's body is wired. When the rapist is hitting her or forcing himself into her, her body releases serious amounts of oxytocin to protect itself and her body. After a rape, the girl thinks that she is weird that she became wet when the guy was raping her. She might think she is damaged goods, unacceptable to 'normal' men. Totally wrong. All girls are hard wired the same way. There is no way to change those nerves and hormones. Role-playing can help her deal with a past rape or prepare against the worse if it ever happened to her.

The male in bondage, experiences being submissive to his loved one, an emotion he normally never experiences. As much as he loves his girl, men are wired into thinking that they know best and that they are in charge. Letting your man experience being submissive to your will might even be good for your relationship. The id of his personality will have to acknowledge at some level that you are often in charge. Granted it is a bit late to be trying to change your man, but it is fun trying! If you can get him to acknowledge his submissive side, he will be far easier to live with!

Doris

I loved Doris more than life itself. She was perfect. A cute face, divine hair, legs that went all the way up and back again and were flexible enough to twist in an amazing number of configurations. Her personality was designed for love. We both were in college at the time and we loved to go to our college team's Saturday night games. She made a vow that each time our team scored, we had to kiss. It didn't seem to matter what I thought. She decided for the two of us! Our team was good so we kissed a lot.

Doris was holding out for marriage. *(Hey, this was a long time ago!)* But she felt kissing was allowed. And she could kiss! I don't know how she did it. Maybe it was just because I was much younger then. But I had kissed many girls before; none of them could hold a flame to Doris.

I think it was because she put her whole mind and soul into it, not expecting sex after, the kiss was what it was all about. She taught me more about kissing than I had any right to know at such an early age. She taught me that it wasn't about mashing your lips together. It was about communication.

When kissing me she was telling me in her kiss, "I am the most passionate girl you will ever meet. I am the girl you want to spend the rest of your life with. I am yours, just say the word. I am yours, body and soul."

God, I was hooked! Her kisses were so sweet. The promise of her kisses was so desirable. I wanted her so much. So did another guy. She married someone else. I lost out. She was lost to me.

I still remember the sweetness of her kisses. I will to my dying day. She taught me to say, "Yes!" when given a choice. Don't hesitate. Don't hesitate like I did.

Chapter Eight
Viagra

Viagra and its clones, Cialis and Levitra, have revolutionized growing old. There is now a reason to get up in the morning, or rather go to bed at night! Unfortunately, not everything is coming up roses. Yes, the man gets hard. The problem is that Viagra works by opening up the veins and arteries so the penis can be adequately fed by an ample blood supply. However, his penis still won't get rock hard if his brain is not flooding his bloodstream with testosterone. Bummer. Women are still going to have to seduce their men to get laid! I know men are supposed to do the seducing but if you wait for them to get around to it, you will never get any action. It was different when you were single. Men fought to sit next to you. Now that you are married to a 60+ man, he just fights to sit next to the TV! No wonder you are thinking about an affair!

Sometimes your man doesn't pursue you as actively as he used to, as he is afraid he might not be able to perform, he is worried he won't be able to get a hard on. This happens to all men once in a while, *(probably after eating lots of red meat or bananas. See the last chapter!)* If it happens three times in a row, or no matter what you do, he just never gets rock hard; it is time to look into Viagra, Cialis Levitra and the new man on the block, Staxyn.

They are wonder drugs. They really work and now that they are so popular, the cost is much more reasonable. If you buy them in bulk, *(is there any other way?)* the cost is less than a buck a pill. Well worth the price to get a bit of action! Cheaper than wine!

So how do they work? Like men, it's complicated. I'll try to keep it simple. First, Viagra. *(Viagra lost its patent in March of 2012, which is why all these cheap Viagra pills are flooding the market.)* When the brain gets sexually excited, it sends a signal down to the area around the artery that feeds blood to the penis. The nerve cell produces nitric oxide which directs the area around the artery to make an enzyme called cGMP. *(cyclic guanosine monophosphate)* cGMP tells the artery to relax and allow more blood to flow. All these enzymes we are going to be talking about are made out of testosterone.

The body always has checks and balances so the nerve is also producing PDE. *(phosphodiesterase)* PDE destroys cGMP almost as fast as it is produced. Not to worry. The brain is making sure that more is being produced as long as it *(the brain)* is sexually excited. When the brain hears a radio with the sports news outside your window, his brain forgets about creating cGMP and PDE destroys all the left over cGMP and the erection disappears. Viagra, on the other hand, destroys PDE so the brain can hear the sports news and the body happily keeps making love.

There are always side affects. The chemical Viagra uses *(sildenafil citrate)* also affects the retina and messes up the user's color vision especially the blue green spectrum. *(You see everything in a blue haze, so your girl didn't just turn into an alien!)* If you take nitroglycerine for your heart, know that it works the same as Viagra. It can confuse the poor little heart. For me the worse is Viagra also opens up arteries in the brain's lining giving the user a massive headache. If a young person uses Viagra, it can become habit forming and he won't be able to get an erection without the pill. These side effects don't happen to everyone, but if they happen to you, now you know why.

Cialis and Levitra work exactly the same way as Viagra but use different chemicals and so have different side effects. Cialis causes muscle aches and back pain. *(Viagra lasts 4 hours, Levitra 5 hours, Cialis lasts a day and a half; which is why it is called the 'Weekender!')* Fatty foods, like red meat and butter on your baked potato, reduce the affect of Viagra and Levitra but have no affect on Cialis.

Which ever you choose, if you choose, know that it only works if your system is flooded with testosterone first. Seduce your man. Make sure he knows you want him. Tell him that his is the only body that can get you off. Lie. He won't know. He will believe you. Men are really weird! And Complicated!

Natasha

Natasha came to me late in life. I was 37 when I met her. I had half decided that life had passed me by. OK. Not life. I had experienced lots of that! But life with one girl. One very special girl. I knew what I wanted. And I searched. Year after year, I searched. Seemingly in vain. I found lots of girls. Lots of Wild Wahines. But not the one I wanted.

I finally found her in the wilds of Papua New Guinea. She was an American who became a Kiwi who was teaching school on a primitive island so far away from civilization they didn't even have international news on the radio. I was passing through on my boat heading for Australia and stopped to let the cyclone season pass by.

It was love at first sight. Why this one and not so many others? What was so special about Natasha? I had known so many girls. Experienced so much. How could I pick one out of the multitude?

To this day, I cannot say for sure why. I looked into her eyes and she in mine and something clicked. It was enough to make one believe in past lives. Was she a lost lover of centuries gone by that I had been looking for these many years?

All I know is I looked into her eyes and my whole being shouted, "Yes!" I don't know why my inner being suddenly became so vocal. It had never shouted out before. Did something or someone awaken it?

It has been twenty five years now and still every day we make wild passionate love. Everyday we gaze into each other's eyes and smile in love and desire and joy. Maybe it is true that there is a special one out there for everyone. I don't know about that. I do know that I found my special one. My princess. My sweetheart. My lover. My one and only. My bride. My Natasha.

Conclusion

Men are very complicated. It can be very confusing to live with one of them. And it's hell if you have an extra one on the side. Very frustrating at times. Enough to drive you around the bend. But I will let you in on a little secret. A man who has just been laid, is easy to live with, a man who is satisfied sexually is a pleasure to spend your life with. It isn't difficult. You can do it! You know how now.

Men like to get their rocks off, as it is so quaintly described. But even more, they love to make their ladies orgasm. It makes them feel like real men if they can make their woman have the deep throated, eyes unfocused, head thrown back, orgasm of incredible joy. Often men have given up, as nothing they do seems to work. It isn't that they don't want to make you come, they do, but they have given up trying.

You have to teach them your special places. Patiently, nicely, sweetly, full of laughter and mingled with joy. If you can, if you can teach your man each of your erogenous zones, if you can conquer your shyness and play with each of his, the man you were thinking about divorcing will become the man of your dreams. Really! You loved him once. He just gave up trying.

When men reach their 60th birthday, a little voice in the back of their head is telling them that their sex life is all over. Don't accept that from your guy. You are in your prime. Now is when you have the time for sex. Kids are gone, soon he will be retired. You might even have the money for romantic vacations. If he tries to give up on sex, don't let him. It isn't fair. It isn't fair for him and it definitely isn't fair for you. You have been working for this time your whole life. You are just going to have to educate him about all the different ways of making love. Even if he can't get it up, he will still want to make you orgasm. Plus the internet is flooded with pills! When you teach him about all the different ways to do it, he is going to become so excited that the phoenix will be reborn!

Life is about the joy we find in each other. We are the otters of the universe. There is a lot of joy in helping others, especially in helping them to enjoy a full life of sexual fulfillment. Actually it is only fair, if you can teach him to orgasm at his advanced age, he certainly should be polite enough to make your golden years, glowingly satisfied.

The End
Of This Book
But
The Beginning of
The Best Years of Your Life!

www.ingramcontent.com/pod-product-compliance
Lightning Source LLC
Chambersburg PA
CBHW060717030426
42337CB00017B/2909